Musings of a Networking Maven

A Practical Guide to Self-Awareness and Business Networking Skills

Esther Deutsch

DISCLAIMER:

This book contains the opinions and ideas of the author. The purpose of this book is to provide you with helpful information. This book should not be relied upon solely to make decisions in your business. Careful attention has been paid to ensure the accuracy of the information, but the author cannot assume responsibility for the validity or consequences of its use. This information is not intended to be all things to all business networkers. It is, by nature, generic to most business networkers in general.

The material in this book is for informational purposes only. As each individual situation is unique, the author disclaims responsibility for any adverse effects that may result from the use or application of the information contained in this book. Any use of the information found in this book is the sole responsibility of the reader. Any suggestions found in this book are to be followed only after consultation with your own trusted advisors.

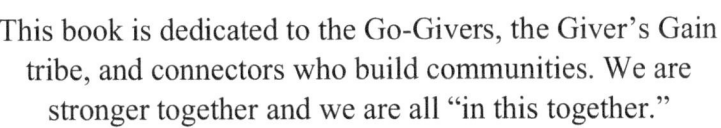

This book is dedicated to the Go-Givers, the Giver's Gain tribe, and connectors who build communities. We are stronger together and we are all "in this together."

"Leadership is a stance in the world. It's not a job title."

Go forth and connect!

CONTENTS

PART 1: WELCOME 1

    INTRODUCTION 3

    WHO SHOULD READ THIS BOOK? 7

    MY PROMISE TO YOU 9

    DO I NEED A BUSINESS NETWORK? 11

PART 2: A CONVERSATION WITH ESTHER
DEUTSCH 17

PART 3: IN THIS TOGETHER ROUNDTABLE 49

    IN THIS TOGETHER ROUNDTABLE ("ITTR") 51

    WHY WE ARE DIFFERENT 51

        OPENNESS 51

        INTEGRITY 51

        PRODUCTIVITY 51

        FAMILY 52

    OUR LEADERSHIP 52

        LUKE VAN EVERY, CO-FOUNDER 52

        ESTHER DEUTSCH, CO-FOUNDER 52

        PJ EWING, MARKETING & MEMBERSHIP 53

    GET IN TOUCH! 54

    ITTR PODCAST/RADIO SHOW DIRECTORY 54

PART 4: FOCUS ON CHARITY 57

    SHEPHERD CENTER 59

    THE HOPE BOX 59

OPERATION PAW 60

FURRY FRIENDS ADOPTION 60

SOCIETY OF WOMEN CODERS 60

BELEV ECHAD 61

JUST CLOWNING AROUND 62

UNITED HATZALAH OF ISRAEL 62

JEWISH NATIONAL FUND 63

SPECIAL OLYMPICS OF NEW YORK 63

BBYO 63

WOMEN'S ENTREPRENEUR CONFERENCE 64

LEUKEMIA & LYMPHOMA SOCIETY 65

CHILDREN'S HARBOR 65

SAVE A SUIT 65

FREADOM PROMOTIONS 66

2030 OR BUST 66

BOYS TO MEN MENTORING VIRGINIA 67

TECHGIRLZ 67

PCS FOR PEOPLE 68

STEIGMANN PEACE AND TOLERANCE
EDUCATION FUND 68

PART 5: THE PATH FORWARD 71

THE NEXT STEP 73

ABOUT ESTHER DEUTSCH 79

ESTHER's CONTACT DETAILS: 80

PART 1: WELCOME

NOTES

_____

_____

_____

_____

_____

_____

_____

_____

_____

_____

_____

_____

_____

_____

_____

_____

_____

_____

_____

_____

_____

_____

INTRODUCTION

Welcome networkers, connectors, and anyone who believes in building relationships in business and in life.

I wrote this book to help you find the resources you need to build self-awareness and enhance your business networking skills.

It is very important for me to share up front that I do not believe that I am an expert networker, whatever that means. You see, I love networking and I love sharing my ideas with others. I am not here to convince anyone that they should be leveraging networking. However, if someone wants to get better at networking, we can play along together.

I will be sharing my insights, ideas, ideals, and resources with you. My goal is to uncover the best of the best resources related to building self-awareness and enhancing your business networking skills.

My hope is that this book will be your guide to building a business network with intention that will serve you, your community, and your business.

The focus of this book will be to share ideas as to how you can focus on building self-awareness and enhancing your business networking skills.

I will share my philosophy in this book and some strategies you can implement on your own. You can reach out to me if you like my philosophy. And I am perfectly fine if you choose to work on building self-awareness and enhancing your business networking skills on your own.

You can reach out to me directly at any time if you want more guidance based on what I am sharing with you in this book. The first step in working with me is to join one of our In This Together Roundtable Sessions.

If we both agree that we might be a good fit to work together, the next step is to schedule a Strategy Session. The goal of the Strategy Session is very simple – to determine if we are a mutual fit to work together. You can reach out to me at any time to schedule a Strategy Session.

We will cover a few things in this book:

- Sharing my networking philosophy.
- Exploring the mindset necessary to enhance your business networking skills.
- Exploring the skill set necessary to improve your business networking skills.
- Exploring the gear set necessary to enhance your business networking skills.
- How to have a deeper impact with both your existing and new connections.
- How to network smarter, not harder.

I want to keep this book short and to the point.

To your success!

Esther Deutsch

https://estherdeutsch.com

https://www.linkedin.com/in/esther-deutsch

NOTES

_____

_____

_____

_____

_____

_____

_____

_____

_____

_____

_____

_____

_____

_____

_____

_____

_____

_____

_____

_____

_____

NOTES

_____

_____

_____

_____

_____

_____

_____

_____

_____

_____

_____

_____

_____

_____

_____

_____

_____

_____

_____

_____

_____

_____

_____

WHO SHOULD READ THIS BOOK?

I wrote this book for business networkers and connectors who want to get better at building an intentional business network. I want to share my lessons and musings as I learned how to build self-awareness and enhance my business networking skills.

You should read this book if:

- You are in some way responsible for adding revenues to a business.
- You love networking and want to get better at it.
- You want to network smarter, not harder.
- You believe that building a network is a great path to success in any endeavor.
- You view networking as the path to building a better business and also a better world.

I will share my best advice on how to build self-awareness and enhance your business networking skills. I will also be sharing resources to guide you on your journey to improve your mindset, skill set, and gear set.

Whether we work together or not, I encourage you to take the time to read this book and see if there are any strategies that can have a positive impact on your business or life right now.

I have intentionally left many blank pages for you to use to take notes as you cultivate your business network.

A good portion of this book is written in a question-and-answer format. I want you to be able to jump to the questions that interest you the most. There is no one right way to read this book.

What part of this resonates with you? Why do you want to continue reading this book?

_____

_____

_____

_____

_____

_____

_____

How important is it to you start building self-awareness and enhancing your business networking skills? Why?

_____

_____

_____

_____

_____

_____

_____

_____

MY PROMISE TO YOU

If you are still with me, I promise not to waste your time. Quite the contrary, I truly hope this book gives you options and inspiration when it comes to building self-awareness and enhancing your business networking skills.

We will be updating this book on a regular basis. We welcome your feedback so that we can create a valuable resource for the business networking community.

NOTES

_____

_____

_____

_____

_____

_____

_____

_____

_____

_____

_____

_____

_____

_____

_____

_____

_____

_____

_____

_____

_____

_____

DO I NEED A BUSINESS NETWORK?

We offer this simple diagnostic to help you determine whether you want to initiate a project on your own to focus on building self-awareness and enhancing your business networking skills.

These questions should guide your decision and give you clarity.

You probably do not need my help if you answer yes to most of these questions. However, if you answered no or maybe, you probably need my help. Even if you answered yes to every question, you may wish to have my help so that you can fast-track your business networking skills.

Question	Yes	Maybe	No
Am I self-aware and conscious of the way I interact with others?			
Do I know with certainty how to add new connections to my personal network in the quantity I need to realize my goals?			
Do I know with certainty how to earn referrals from my existing business network?			
Do I know with certainty how to optimize my business network?			
Do I know with certainty how to maximize the effectiveness of my business network?			
Is my networking leading me to feel more fulfilled? Hint: It should!			

What questions do you have for yourself as you go through this initial diagnostic?

_____

_____

_____

_____

_____

_____

_____

_____

_____

_____

_____

_____

_____

_____

_____

_____

_____

_____

_____

NOTES

_____

_____

_____

_____

_____

_____

_____

_____

_____

_____

_____

_____

_____

_____

_____

_____

_____

_____

_____

NOTES

_____

_____

_____

_____

_____

_____

_____

_____

_____

_____

_____

_____

_____

_____

_____

_____

_____

_____

_____

NOTES

NOTES

_____

_____

_____

_____

_____

_____

_____

_____

_____

_____

_____

_____

_____

_____

_____

_____

_____

_____

_____

_____

PART 2: A CONVERSATION WITH ESTHER DEUTSCH

NOTES

_____

_____

_____

_____

_____

_____

_____

_____

_____

_____

_____

_____

_____

_____

_____

_____

_____

_____

_____

_____

_____

_____

This section has deliberately been written in conversational form. I chose this format for two reasons:

1. I am a friendly person; I prefer a conversation to a lecture.
2. I wanted to show that I have these conversations all the time and I wanted you to benefit from being part of the conversation.

Let's dive in!

Let's focus on telling the story of Esther the Connector. What is the essence of Esther?

Most people have no idea about the value of an intentionally created business network. I realize now that my network is valuable to anybody I work with, including those who I include in my network.

I realized that networking is as natural to me as breathing. It is sometimes hard to explain to others "how" I network.

I will try to share my essence in this conversation.

I am currently training employees and trying to show them my networking tips so that they can apply them to their own business development activities.

I will be honest with you, there are some things that to me are just there - I don't know how I know them. I don't remember a time when I didn't do these things naturally.

I will try to share the natural skills that I have acquired in hopes that it benefits the reader.

What would you say to someone who says that you shouldn't monetize networking?

This is a common statement in networking. There are those who believe it is wrong to in some way make money through networking. I respond with a question, "why shouldn't I monetize my God given gifts?"

To be clear, I will happily help someone who needs to meet someone in my network. However, I also spend a lot of time, energy, and money building my network with intention.

People who want free access to my network are not recognizing the value that a good relationship building brings to the conversation.

Esther, why don't you just share a little bit about who you are and what you do?

I am a social worker by education, but I work in a very corporate role right. I work for a technology and cybersecurity company.

I am overseeing talent acquisition, sales, and marketing. I am also doing some community building both internally and externally, with our partners.

I also do a lot of public speaking, I do a lot of coaching, even some consulting.

I also consult for a company called Market Intent.ai, which is a data and technology marketing startup (https://marketintent.ai).

Esther, please share a little bit about why you believe in networking so much.

I really appreciate meeting like-minded people, and that's what it's about, right? It's about finding those people that you connect with, and you know, going further together. So that's really my why, that's really it.

What does networking mean to you versus community building?

I see them as being somewhat overlapping because every community is made up of individual people. By networking, you are building relationships. That's a big part of building community as well.

Letting people know that they matter and figuring out why. Asking them what you can give to them and what they offer and showing them their strengths.

I think it's similar skills that we use in networking and community building and even Leadership Development.

Honestly, the term "networking" is really overused or abused. I don't know what the best word is, but people maybe get worried or nervous when they think of networking.

Networking is in essence simple. It's about meeting other people and finding a connection. Like it's really connection.

Connection is important with building a community too. They're sort of synergistic and maybe work together, but a little bit different in application.

One way that I distinguish the two is that I consider networking to be one to one. Most networking mentors on the planet teach us how to be amazing one on one networkers.

With community building, we are removing the "one" from it, and it is really many to many.

That is where a community starts to become a three-dimensional living breathing organism, rather than a whole bunch of people in a database.

The way that it has worked for me is that through networking, if you network enough and consistently, you actually build a community of people who may not know each other, but who you know, and their community knows one another through you.

It's kind of a weird thing, but that is part of the power of the one to one and building that sort of relationship.

Eventually, your network grows on its own and frankly takes on a life of its own. This is similar to community building.

I've done a lot of community building in my past life, and I actually take an approach to making it individual and the community is really made up of individual people just like a business.

You're not selling to a business; you're selling to the people in the organization. So, it's really they're both sort of interchangeable but different.

What does relationship building mean to you?

This is a hard question to answer for me, but I would say that it really means understanding and being curious and learning about other people and what drives them and how what you offer benefits them.

What drives them, to me, is a little bit about what their past is, where they want to go, what's important to them, what they are looking to accomplish, etc. Whether it's through our conversation in life or in business, or both, then I want to figure out how I can use myself (or my network) to help further their agenda.

I love helping them get where they want to go.

To me, it is a high level of self-awareness as well as being curious and open and being able to be receptive to the person you're engaging with. I try to always focus on where the other person wants to go and starting there before starting, with myself.

A lot of people who are new to networking are probably confused right now. If you are putting the needs of others ahead of yourself, what's in it for you?

Absolutely fair. I think that that's a big challenge that many people must overcome with networking. And sometimes I find myself getting stuck in that trap of "what's in it for me?"

It also has to do with recognizing that networking is not a short game. It's a long game and it's not transactional if you want to do it right.

In my book, networking is not transactional most of the time. To be clear, it can occasionally be transactional, but that's not what I call networking. That's what I call having a transaction between two people.

Think of it like a friendship, right? You're not going to go to somebody you just met and say, "Hey, can you buy from me right now? Or can you give me something right now?"

Because chances are you're not going to be friends much longer if you don't work on long term and build that foundation first.

Focus on building that relationship and then the rest will come.

A lot of people want transactions right now. But the problem is if you focus on getting a transaction from a person, then you must run around and find the next person for the next transaction.

Whereas, if you build relationships first, the next transaction just naturally appears because you've got that connection.

Can you share an example as to how your network can help others?

I have a friend who is working on a project. There is absolutely nothing in it for me. But I sent it out to my network anyway. I basically said "Hey, everybody, I have a friend working on this project, who knows somebody that can help?"

In the end, somebody will be able to assist my friend. And she will remember me for helping her out.

I try to be very mature in my networking. I know that might sound a bit judgy for those who don't network the way I do. But I think that's the secret to networking. It's not like there's a scarcity mindset of "here's a transaction for you, give me one back."

It is more about how we serve one another, and we're all better for it.

And, if it's something that plays into your networking skills are useful for making life better for someone else, it carries over into other areas of your network.

Abundance is a huge part of my networking essence. If you are somebody who sees abundance in the world, then it's going to translate to your networking too.

Test out the power of networking. Maybe you have something in your personal life that you are working on. Find a way to be more giving, more generous, and think about putting the people around you (spouses, kids, whatever) ahead of your needs. Think about how you can give value to them and think about them before yourself. This will translate into your networking and vice versa.

How can I become a better networker?

Something that people don't realize is that the best way to be a great networker is to spend as much as half of your time serving others. That might mean that you are looking for opportunities for someone else while you are looking for your next opportunity.

I love finding people who are good people and who have value to offer and ways or resources that you can share with your network. This is not about finding direct business for yourself.

It's a powerful tool that people forget. Look for people who can help people in your network, not just directly refer business to you.

What is in it for you?

I get asked this a lot, usually by people who don't fully understand the power of a great network.

In the more evolved networking communities, as a collective, we all know a lot of people.

It is not uncommon for me to reach out and ask, "Hey, I need somebody in Florida who happens to know how to prune a specific type of tree." Somebody in my network will respond and tell me who to send them to.

You ask me what is in it for me. Well, I made someone else's day better. Tomorrow, they're going to remember me and they're going to find a way to make my day better. By the way, it doesn't have to be that direct. It just might be enough to know that someday I will need help and they will respond kindly by helping me. Or they may pay it forward by helping a random stranger.

I don't do it for the immediate benefit, to me it is about that long-term relationship, not about an immediate transaction.

Talking about translating networking into a benefit, I believe that if you have a desire to help somebody, even if it doesn't seem doable on paper, that there's a way for you to do that directly. There will be an opportunity either now or down the road to do so, in some way, shape or form.

So, we'll just put that out there for the universe.

How do you actively and intentionally build relationships?

One of the best ways to build relationships is to introduce people in my network to one another. I give before ever asking for anything in return.

I think about building relationships a lot because I want to be able to share my secrets. I want everybody out there to be able to network like myself and others in my network.

There is no exclusivity on networking well. The more people who do it well, the more we all win. Remember my abundance mindset?

I share my relationship building tips freely and still many people don't do it. Don't be one of those people. Please take note and implement some of these tips.

You will see the changes and I want you to be successful.

My number one secret is something very few people want to do. The first thing you must do is **care**.

Building relationships will be a challenge for you if you don't care about others. And it sounds silly, but it's nuanced. When you are speaking to somebody who doesn't care, you will feel it and you will know. And, if you don't care, others will know it too.

A simple example, if someone tells you they only have thirty minutes for a conversation, make sure you end on time. Going overtime, even just by a minute, might cause a problem for them. Not caring about that is going to be a problem for you.

Not caring will be challenging in building relationships. When you're the person engaging in this connection, you don't want to be feeling that sort of negative energy.

Great networkers tend to have a lot of interests and a lot of demands on their time. Don't waste their time!

I would also say that you need to be **curious**. You need to be curious about others. In my experience, every single person has something that you can learn from them.

Sometimes it is how to do something, other times you can learn what not to do. Either way, that is still valuable to you, right? That's still a lesson we can learn from someone.

Mindset is extremely important. One of the things that I like to do is every time I walk into space, and that could be a virtual meeting on Zoom not just a physical room, I try to think about what I can contribute to the meeting. I want to know that if I wasn't there, my contribution wouldn't be there either.

I would love it if everybody did this little exercise before entering a networking event or any kind of event around relationship building. Ask yourself, "what makes me unique?"

Self-awareness is critical to this, and it is my third secret. Your self-awareness is directly correlated to how well you will network and serve others. Do you know what you have to offer that can make someone else's day better?

Often, the only thing that I can offer someone new is a smile. I will challenge you to pick one person to do something nice for in every social interaction you have.

Your kindness matters, because, for that person, if you weren't there, they might not have had that connection.

Caring, curiosity, and self-awareness are the not-so-little things that make a big difference between someone who is successful at building relationships and someone who is struggling.

A nice side benefit is that these ingredients can also make a positive difference in the world.

I can't stress this enough, the best networkers that I know are very self-aware. They know exactly what they are looking for, what their emotional triggers are, what annoys them, and what interests them.

I want to circle back to the word curiosity. A lot of people try to learn how to network, but they don't understand how important curiosity about others can be. In my world, there is a lesson in every person I have ever met.

Is your level of self-awareness something that people can cultivate or is that something that you must be born with?

Self-awareness (and caring and curiosity) are one hundred percent something that people can cultivate.. I recommend Brené Brown's works as a good place to start.

I personally am far from where I hope to be in my own self-awareness down the road. Self-awareness is something that I am actively working on. Even just being aware of the need for self-awareness is helpful.

There is always room to grow in every area for everybody. Of course, me included, you can absolutely cultivate personal growth.

There are amazing books, workshops, mentors, and role models.

I do a lot of assessments regularly on myself. Every day, I am learning about others and continue to be curious about myself.

For example, when it comes to love, you can't give it to others until you have it for yourself (and give it to yourself).

I have self-surprises all the time. Maybe I didn't know that I like a specific food or and maybe I didn't like it back in the day, but maybe I like it now.

I know myself and then I really don't.

But just recognizing being aware, knowing when the surprises occur and crop up, and then finding different resources to work on myself.

This little practice can help you get better with your self-awareness.

Having a mentor or talking to somebody else who sees your blind spots is powerful, even if you see them as an equal.

You don't have to pursue gurus or TED speakers, because you might not have access to somebody like that. It doesn't matter who you learn from, if it is somebody who is more objective than you are. It is very hard to be objective when we are looking at ourselves.

There is something powerful that has stuck with me. Unfortunately, I forget where I first saw this. There is book where they asked a friend "if you weren't afraid of me getting upset and I had no emotion involved, what would you tell me about myself?"

What the friend told them started to make the person feel bad about themselves, like they were under attack. After the person had a moment of self-reflection, their perspective changed. They were so grateful that this person had given them insights.

As I read it, I remember asking myself "Who do I have in my life that I can ask this to?"

I really wanted to learn more about what I need to work on because I care, and I want to be a better person. I want to be better for myself and for others. Acknowledging that we all have room to grow and improve shouldn't be a shameful act. It's a human one and something I believe we are all here to do.

It shouldn't be offensive to you if you are asking the right person and you really care about becoming a better person. Hopefully, they will share something that you can work on. I am working on my own self-awareness right now. Improving our self-awareness is a learned behavior.

Is it fair to say that with self-awareness, we can recognize that feedback can either be something to be offended by or it can be a precious gift? We get to choose how we take things. Somebody is risking their status with you in a relationship to tell you what they would improve about you. Self-awareness starts with a seed, and it can grow, but that is not going to happen overnight, it takes time.

If I can contradict myself for a second, I want to put out a little caveat.

There are times where people will give you advice or tell you things about yourself that don't come from a place of strength and may not be true for your situation.

There is a counterbalance, only you know yourself. I have been guilty of this, taking criticism from someone else too seriously.

Only you are in your exact circumstances and know exactly what you need to do. We all have the answers inside ourselves if we get the right advice and direction and then reapply it. Deep in our hearts, we know what we need to do.

There are checks and balances. I say this because I created not for profits back in the day. Had I listened to some of the advice that I had gotten or people telling me I was crazy or don't do it, it would never have happened. I followed my dreams and many, many hundreds of lives were positively impacted as a result.

At that time, I did have doubts, I did it anyway.

When I look back, I think that I shouldn't have had certain doubts and should have done things differently, because I knew in my heart what I needed to do.

Sometimes it is important to be careful about where you get your advice. Make sure you get it from the right people. Find someone who is looking to lift you up and elevate you and help you become a better person.

Sometimes you take the advice and then you decide this isn't right for you now for whatever reason, and that's fine.

I always try to say "thank you so much for the advice" whether it had an immediate impact on me or not. The idea is to get the advice and to reflect on it and to see how it might apply. Maybe it is not good, and you will feel like it's a mistake.

Doing the work to carefully consider the advice you receive is important. Try to have some kind of checks and balances.

It is also about being honest with yourself and knowing when to listen to others and when not to.

What are some practical things that people who might not be completely self-aware yet can do to build relationships while they are doing their inner work to improve their own self-awareness?

Other areas of networking or relationship building that I want to talk about are **preparation and follow up**.

It is sad that so much of our effort and a lot of the material out there is focused on the actual relationship building and how to conduct those conversations and how to make networking work.

It is not an exaggeration to say that ninety-nine percent of success in networking is in the preparation and follow up specifically.

I say this all the time and so few people do it. Sorry, but that is why they are failing. I say that confidently, you are not building relationships if you are not doing proper preparation and follow up.

Here is an extreme example. You might meet someone on the street and hit it off immediately. You might have an amazing conversation. You might think that you are forever friends connected to the soul. But, if you don't reach out again, and they don't reach out to you, it doesn't matter that you connected in the first place. You may as well have never met them. And you also just as well have never gone to the event or engaged in that one conversation.

When I meet somebody, I am already thinking about the future. The first conversation is only like an interview. It's a lead into the next one. And that's really all I care about. It's creating a connection so that we want to talk again.

Your preparation is epic. What is your process for preparation? How do you prepare to meet a new friend?

Process is a great way to describe what I do because it is practical. I want my preparation to be practical.

Honestly, it is very hard to say generically how I do my preparation, because it depends on whether it's in person or online.

One example of something I do as soon as I get a connection to somebody or I'm in touch with them is to go right to their social media. For me, it is LinkedIn. For you, it might be something else based on your environment.

I connect with the person right away. A lot of people don't do that until they have the first conversation. Not a good idea! Right now, I have already brought them into my world by connecting with them. I have already started building this foundation for our relationship before we speak.

That's the first thing, and I will send them a message saying, "so great to connect with you in this place or in that city or through this person's connection."

That's twofold.

First, it is completely selfish so that in three years (because I'm in it for the long run) when I go back to reconnect with them, and to do my touch points, I know where I met them. You might not think this is important if you only know five people. But, if you continue to follow my advice and tips, you are going to meet a million people from all over the world. You want to be able to keep that connection alive, and this is how you do it.

Second, for their benefit. If they are an amazing networker and have a huge community, you want them to be able to know where or how they first got connected to you.

Also, if I have the ability, I will try to find out some information about them. I understand that people have time constraints. There is only so much research you can do, but it could be as easy as taking two minutes. Everybody has two minutes before you have a new conversation where you can learn something about them.

What do they care about? What are they putting out to the world? Even if there is nothing that tells you something about them. Maybe the value you are going to give them is as simple as showing them how they can put out more information for the world so that people can find them for the amazing service that they have to offer.

Find whatever insight you can and take note that even "no information" is also information. Everything you uncover matters.

You might also find that you have a similar interest, background, education, passion, or something. You might Google them and find out that you both played Little League in school.

There is so much you could do before the conversation even happens to facilitate where you want to go and where they want to go.

That is where I start. It is almost like dating, right? You are in the dating stage. You are getting to learn about each other.

The way that you respond to your email is important. Do you add value to your initial engagement? There is always an opportunity to add value right away and you all should be thinking about what you can add to their world.

Once you join the meeting, how do you greet them? Do you thank them for meeting you? Are you generous? Are you gracious? If you need to reschedule your meeting, how do you do so? Do you apologize for having to change things and extend the same grace to them?

What are you giving them to give them the idea that this is somebody that they want to connect with?

Those are the things that I am thinking about before meeting someone.

One of the big "aha" moments for me, is the value that we bring to our network by being a connector. Every time you introduce somebody to me, when people are connected and you connect the right people, expressing gratitude is a currency that elevates everybody in the equation. What do you do to follow up because every single introduction you make to me is a love fest for you? Everybody I meet tells me how amazing you are, and I do the same.

I'll first speak to follow up.

I just want to go to the actual engagement first. Part of my other goal in the initial meeting is to get another meeting and to continue the relationship.

I truly want to earn one or more interactions. I do that by looking for more great things that the person is looking for now that I can fulfill. That is my goal.

Hopefully in your conversation this will come out naturally if you are looking for it. Usually, you will find it if you are looking for it.

What's the easiest way to find out what a person needs? It could be nothing, but it could be they will say nothing. Don't assume. Ask, ask, and ask again!

For example, if we had a great conversation. It was awesome, we talked about pizza because we both love pizza. I am so glad, and my pizza game is now elevated forever because of what you share with me.

The one thing I did get to learn is I know what topics to let you know about in the future. Perhaps I didn't get to learn what I could do to help you yet, I will ask "How can I add value to you today?"

To be clear, it is not going to be that I can send you a client today because we just met, and I don't know anyone off the top of my head.

There are many other ways I might be able to help you. What are you looking for? What do you need?

Just ask, and most of the time people will have something that you might not even have uncovered if you didn't ask or sometimes, they'll say nothing or they'll say something, and you can ask a follow up question.

Well, from what I heard in our conversation, you love pizza. I know a great spot; can I send you a slice? Or how about a recommendation?

You can always give something. Hopefully, it is something that you know is related to what you're looking to get.

Now it goes one step further. Don't just say you are going to do it. This is a very personal thing. I like to do things right away. I am a doer. Do it right away because that is the best way to build trust and credibility.

Make sure you keep your word, which is crucial in building relationships.

I like to leave time after calls (and sometimes I don't leave enough time) to complete what I have promised. I will tell the person a timeline to set expectations. Maybe I am going to be away for the next two weeks. I will tell them that it is going to take me two weeks to do something. I always ask if the timeline is okay with them. Of course, they will say yes.

Here's the catch. You could say six months. Make sure you do it in six months, or else you're better off not having the conversation.

I can't say it strongly enough and it sounds silly, but people don't follow up like that.

And the way I remember to do something in six months is to use a task reminder in my CRM (Customer Relationship Manager). There are many great free CRM tools out there if you don't have one already. Make yourself a note to follow up, because you are human and you can't remember everything off the top of your head, no matter how few connections you have, because it's six months away.

And I assume follow up and reminders is even more important as your network grows?

I was going to say that. I want everyone to know that follow up is relevant for everybody at any stage of relationship building.

Even if you have two commitments to two connections, you are human and you need to create a follow up system for yourself. That is the respectful thing to do because you made a promise to somebody, and you need to fulfill it. Even if you leave your job, it is your responsibility to get their information off LinkedIn or somewhere else and make sure you fulfill the promise that you made to them.

The number one most important aspect of follow up is to always keep your promises.

Can introverts network?

I am an extroverted introvert and I think it's a myth that introverts can't network. Introverts are some of the best networkers around because often they know how to listen, they're thoughtful, they ask good questions, which is a big part of relationship building.

I am working on asking better questions because I don't think I always ask the best questions. Part of getting the best answer is to ask the right question.

I just want to put out there on record that introverts can be great networkers. It is a myth that you need to be a certain this or that to be a good leader, you need to be a certain personality. You do not in fact, it can even be an advantage to be an introvert. It is just knowing how to use your strengths and what types of relationship building to do that feeds who you are.

Again, everything is really connected to that self-awareness we discussed earlier and leveraging your strengths.

I know a lot of introverts who say, "I'm an introvert, therefore, I can't network." I know many introverts who are world class networkers. If you are curious about this, check out the book *Quiet: The Power of Introverts in a World That Can't Stop Talking* by Susan Cain. It blew my mind.

I would say another thing about the follow up, is don't assume things about people. I encounter this a lot and it is pretty mind blowing. A lot of times people assume that you are looking for a specific thing and a conversation or that your need now is a certain thing. I want to repeat this again here. Always ask don't assume.

It's as if you gave on the same level. So, we often give the way that we want to be given. We want to give the way we want to receive. We do this by default instead of understanding the other person and how they want to receive and adapting our way of giving accordingly.

It's an important thing to keep in mind. Always ask, don't assume, ask. "I can make fifteen introductions to you. Is that what you want? Is that what you're looking for? Is that going to be helpful for you now?"

The answer is not always yes, and that matters, it shows that you care by respecting what's important to them, not just what you have, that you want to give.

I have had people complain about getting things that to me would have been a great gift. You must keep in mind the other person, not yourself so much.

How can people make your life easier when they are attempting to connect with you? We want to uplevel the networking community so that people aren't bringing things that they think are gifts that are really annoying. How can people best connect with you and best serve you?

I really appreciate that question.

I am very active on LinkedIn. LinkedIn is one of my favorite platforms to connect with people.

I love meeting new people and being active. I am always open to making new connections there.

Also, you can always find me at our corporate website, which is https://www.rcsprofessional.com or my personal one https://www.estherdeutsch.com.

I love that you asked that question. I personally love it when people come to one of my networking communities before we meet, because again, it gives me time to get to know them in a way that isn't one to one. I actually find value in that long term.

A lot of people don't ask or don't want to know because they want to connect in the way that's best for them. That is fine. But, if they did really want to do it in a way that's best for me, that's what I love most.

I love having more people on my networking groups, I have the ability to meet a lot of people and still be able to connect on an individual level and help them. Meeting in a group saves me some time.

It shows your mindset in helping others the way that they want to be helped.

Who or what resources have inspired and shaped you the most in your networking journey? Who are your big inspirations in your networking style?

I relate most to people who are practical and people who I can see myself in. Not necessarily where I am, sometimes where I want to be.

I learned a lot about relationship building in my training to become a social worker. That was the impetus for my desire to become a social worker. I had an incredible background and an incredible internship experience with a nonprofit called Pathways to Leadership.

We worked in schools doing one to one mentorship with students in schools that had been labeled by the government in New York City as problematic. I was working with middle schoolers, most of them were living in homeless shelters or in the correctional system or both.

I learned more about relationship building than I've ever learned in that one year. I had amazing supervision and one of my mentors I'm still in touch with from that organization. I learned so much because I had to engage students who were struggling so much, and it was such a challenge, but it taught me how to connect with people at their level and achieve a goal.

That is where I found a lot of my inspiration and help. I learn a lot from working with youth in general, if you have an opportunity to do it. From a volunteer standpoint, it's really powerful. You learn a lot because they give it to you as it is. There is no sugarcoating, and you learn a lot about yourself too.

They gave me a lot more than I thought I gave to them. I hope that I gave them a lot back. The students I worked with were a big part of my inspiration.

I revert to this experience even now when I look to turning leads into clients. I went into social work school because I wanted to improve my relationships with people and build better connections. I hope that I have accomplished that. That is a lot of my "why" for what I do in networking.

What are your favorite books for our readers?

I would say two books that I love that are more relationship focused.

Marcus Sheridan is a big thought leader in the marketing space. In my opinion, he is very thoughtful in the relationship building space as well.

The book *They Ask, You Answer* changed my life from a marketing standpoint. I got the opportunity to meet Mr. Sheridan at a conference. He was lovely in person, which I assumed through his writing. He is super approachable, just really the nicest guy.

I really recommend another book, which is also helpful for self-awareness. The book is *Taking Flight* by Merrick Rosenberg. We use that internally in our organization, but it's an amazing tool for individuals as well. It's based on the DISC assessment, so it's helping you get to know your style.

What I love about the way that Merrick breaks it down, is it teaches you not just about yourself, which many of the tests do, it also teaches you how to apply yourself in relation to others. Isn't that what it is all about?

I do have a book on Amazon as well. I must mention that here as well. The book is called *The Invisible Entrepreneur: From Mental Health to Mindset* and it is about mental health and entrepreneurship.

Fun fact: I got to co-author this book with my dear friend: Tabatha Barron who I met through – guess what medium – networking of course! You can find our book on Amazon.

I also look for the best books on relationship building and networking. I look for books on service or leadership, like *Setting the Table* by Danny Meyer. I got to meet him, which was incredible. I am a huge fan.

All these meetings were through relationship building, by the way, but service leadership and anything service-related is where you're going to make the best, most fulfilling relationships, not just the most productive.

Do you have any parting thoughts?

One of the first things I thought of when I was planning this book is that *a stranger is only one conversation away from being a friend.*

I've heard that quote. I should have said it first! But it's something that I keep in mind a lot too, especially when I'm not in the mood to talk to people because I'm an introvert at heart.

I know. It's hard to believe.

NOTES

_____

_____

_____

_____

_____

_____

_____

_____

_____

_____

_____

_____

_____

_____

_____

_____

_____

_____

_____

_____

_____

_____

NOTES

NOTES

_____

_____

_____

_____

_____

_____

_____

_____

_____

_____

_____

_____

_____

_____

_____

_____

_____

_____

_____

_____

_____

PART 3: IN THIS TOGETHER ROUNDTABLE

NOTES

_____

_____

_____

_____

_____

_____

_____

_____

_____

_____

_____

_____

_____

_____

_____

_____

_____

_____

_____

_____

IN THIS TOGETHER ROUNDTABLE ("ITTR")

"Whatever the mind of man can conceive and believe, it can achieve. Thoughts are things! And powerful things at that. When mixed with definiteness of purpose, and burning desire, they can be translated into riches."

~Napoleon Hill

WHY WE ARE DIFFERENT

OPENNESS
Our culture is about acceptance and support. We're here to listen, suggest, and connect. We are open to your business story and are ready to help you build the organization that you seek.

No business categories are closed, we have many people in the same field who respect and support each other. We're not competitive, rather we are there to promote growth and business development.

INTEGRITY
When we share news and programs on the weekly Roundtable Discussion, we are speaking the truth about our business goals and who we want to meet. Our group is founded on trust in each other. And it is this trust that forms the bonds that allow us to network with confidence.

PRODUCTIVITY
We measure our success by relationships formed, connections made, business education, and deals done.

FAMILY

Just like your family we are supportive, generous, and forgiving. You don't have to be at every meeting. You can multitask, eat lunch, keep your business going while attending our meetings. We chose to stay off video just for this reason.

We're not here to be a burden, but rather to deliver ninety minutes of learning, connecting and business building.

OUR LEADERSHIP

LUKE VAN EVERY, CO-FOUNDER

Experienced Sales Consultant with a demonstrated history of working in the human resources industry. Skilled in Microsoft Word, Sales, Sales Operations, and Customer Satisfaction. Strong sales professional. Expert in HR Management, ACA Compliance, Employee Benefits, Strategic HR Services and more.

Luke leads our weekly In This Together Roundtable networking call each Tuesday at 11:00 a.m. ET. He is a brilliant connector and moderator and has been recognized widely for his ability to build solid and useful business relationships.

ESTHER DEUTSCH, CO-FOUNDER

A Social Worker and Ops Manager, Esther is very passionate about leadership development, education, and problem-solving through innovation.

She loves to network and build thriving communities by leading with heart, sparking creativity, and empowering individual team members to unite and take responsibility for collectively spreading an organization's mission and core purpose.

Her experiences include teaching adults and adolescents of all ages and abilities, founding and running multiple not-for-profit organizations, and producing a variety of events and workshops for both the profit and not-for-profit sectors.

Esther currently works in Technology and Operations at RCS Professional Services and teaches part-time at the University level.

Her favorite quote is:

"Leadership is a stance in the world. It's not a job title."

She is a big believer in the power of hard work and commitment. Esther is always up for networking and looks forward to connecting with everyone.

PJ EWING, MARKETING & MEMBERSHIP

PJ's education started at The University of Michigan (BA) and continued at The University of Notre Dame (MBA Marketing).

He worked on major mass market brands at Leo Burnett Advertising and Tracy Locke (McDonald's, Kraft, Pepsi) and then helped build and sell a company called Screen vision.

After years building sales teams selling non-traditional media, he became the Chief Marketing Officer at X10 Therapy where he continues to create marvelous marketing each day.

In addition to that wonderful work, today PJ helps small and medium businesses grow by leveraging his deep knowledge of marketing strategy and practice.

GET IN TOUCH!

We are looking forward to learning about your business in a future meeting.

To join a meeting, register on our LinkedIn Page here:

https://www.linkedin.com/company/in-this-together-roundtable/about

ITTR PODCAST/RADIO SHOW DIRECTORY

Great people, smart thinking, innovative content. Get to know our ITTR members by listening to the many podcasts (and even broadcast radio shows!) created each week by our group. You will find podcasts, radio shows, even a radio station or two for you to explore. Reach out to the hosts directly to get your "15 minutes of fame" as a guest.

https://inthistogetherroundtable.com/ittr-podcast-directory

NOTES

NOTES

_____

_____

_____

_____

_____

_____

_____

_____

_____

_____

_____

_____

_____

_____

_____

_____

_____

_____

_____

_____

_____

PART 4: FOCUS ON CHARITY

NOTES

_____

_____

_____

_____

_____

_____

_____

_____

_____

_____

_____

_____

_____

_____

_____

_____

_____

_____

_____

_____

_____

I would like to highlight charities that mean a lot to me and my network. Part of my personal self-awareness journey has included finding the causes that matter to me and looking for ways I can add value.

One of the best ways I know of to support a local charity is to share their mission with others. Here are a few I support in no particular order. I encourage you to reach out directly to any of these charities that really resonate with you.

SHEPHERD CENTER

According to Wikipedia: "Shepherd Center is a private, not-for profit hospital in Atlanta, Georgia. Founded in 1975, the 152-bed hospital focuses on the medical treatment, research, and rehabilitation for people with spinal cord injury and disease, acquired brain injury, multiple sclerosis, chronic pain, and other neuromuscular problems."

https://www.shepherd.org

THE HOPE BOX

Rescuing Babies, Empowering Women, Uniting Communities. Virtually unnoticed, infants are being discarded, abandoned, or sold for sexual exploitation daily. Some die of neglect while others become trapped in an overwhelmed system.

The most vulnerable in our society need a voice and an advocate.

THE HOPE BOX is filling that role and is working to improve outcomes for abandoned infants.

https://www.thehopebox.org

OPERATION PAW

Located in South Florida, Operation Paw is a cat transport and more. They rescue and take thousands of cats out of Florida to rescue partners all the way to New Hampshire. As part of this they are constantly having to rent cargo vans and the majority of the time have difficulties. They want to buy a van. The van would also be used to aid fifteen other south Florida rescuer groups who save cats and kittens, as well.

http://www.operationpaw.com

FURRY FRIENDS ADOPTION

Their mission is to provide complete care for abused and abandoned dogs and cats, from rescue to medical care, rehabilitation, and placement in a forever home!

https://furryfriendsadoption.org

SOCIETY OF WOMEN CODERS

Empowering girls through Digital Skills, one line of code at a time.

https://www.sowcoders.org

Check out a blog post I wrote about "Teaching Tech in Belize --- What It Taught Me." I found out about this project through Facebook and networking online.

https://www.rcsprofessional.com/blog/2019/07/teaching-tech-in-belize-what-it-taught

BELEV ECHAD

Since the founding of the State of Israel, hundreds of thousands of young Jewish men and women have risked their lives and limbs to protect the Jewish people and ensure the security of the Jewish Homeland. Many of these soldiers sustain physical injuries and even more are left with emotional scars that can be equally debilitating.

Founded in 2009 by Rabbi Uriel Vigler and his wife Shevy, Belev Echad began as an annual tour of New York City, as a gesture of solidarity and support for wounded warriors of the Israel Defense Forces ("IDF"). What started off as a local initiative of the New York Upper East Side Jewish community has now become a global movement dedicated to helping veterans of the IDF reintegrate into civilian life with the love and support they need to thrive.

We are now an essential part of healing, growing beyond just a vibrant community to a close-knit family. Together, we celebrate birthdays, marriages and births, provide resources and support through the big decisions, and show up when times are tough. These courageous young men and women have risked life and limb for the safety of the Jewish Homeland. Our work with these wounded veterans shows our solidarity and gratitude for their enormous sacrifice.

https://belevechad.nyc

JUST CLOWNING AROUND

A community of young professionals who are bringing happiness to the elderly & homebound & changing the world… one smile at a time! This video explains it all.

https://estherdeutsch.com/jca-just-clowning-around

UNITED HATZALAH OF ISRAEL

United Hatzalah of Israel is the largest independent, non-profit, fully volunteer Emergency Medical Service organization that provides the fastest and free emergency medical first response throughout Israel.

United Hatzalah's service is available to all people regardless of race, religion, or national origin.

United Hatzalah has more than 6,500 volunteers around the country, available around the clock – 24 hours a day, 7 days a week, 365 days a year.

With the help of our unique GPS technology and our iconic ambucycles, our average response time is less than 3 minutes across the country and 90 seconds in metropolitan areas.

Our mission is to arrive at the scene as soon as possible and provide the patient with professional and appropriate medical aid until an ambulance arrives, resulting in many more lives saved. We are also first and last responders at every disaster relief initiative worldwide.

https://israelrescue.org

JEWISH NATIONAL FUND

When you donate to Jewish National Fund-USA, you are building a bright, beautiful future for the people and land of Israel.

https://www.jnf.org

SPECIAL OLYMPICS OF NEW YORK

Special Olympics gives people with intellectual disabilities (ID) the confidence they need to succeed, on and off the playing field. For every person helped, there are 13 others in the U.S. waiting on the sidelines to get in the game. Will you give them a chance?

https://support.specialolympics.org

BBYO

BBYO is the leading pluralistic Jewish teen movement aspiring to involve more Jewish teens in more meaningful Jewish experiences. As expressed in our core values, BBYO welcomes Jewish teens of all backgrounds, denominational affiliation, gender, race, sexual orientation, or socioeconomic status, including those with a range of intellectual, emotional, and physical abilities.

With a network of hundreds of chapters across North America and in 60 countries around the world, BBYO reaches nearly 70,000 teens annually and serves as the Jewish community's largest and most valuable platform for delivering fun, meaningful, and affordable experiences that inspire a lasting connection to the Jewish people.

https://bbyo.org

WOMEN'S ENTREPRENEUR CONFERENCE

Our mission is to prove that no matter where a woman is at in her life, it's never too late for her to start or grow her business. Women are drivers of the economy, but unfortunately, the economy often fails to fuel them. Did you know that:

- Female founders only receive 2.2% of $130 billion dollars in VC funding.
- 42% of women report experiencing gender discrimination in business.
- Women lack leadership representation, with only 5% of Standard & Poor composite's 1,500 leadership positions being filled by women.

To top it off, women haven't had a stable environment specifically dedicated to fostering their entrepreneurial spirit that is both affordable and accessible. Until now!

Enter the Women's Entrepreneurship Conference—WEC as our supporters know us by.

WEC is a series of events put on by parent company *Never Too Late to Start* that helps women break down entrepreneurial barriers. We achieve this through masterclass events that feature expert speakers and panelists.

But let's be honest, a day dedicated to learning is pretty dry! WEC knows how to throw a party, which is why every attendee is treated to our signature cocktail and networking party.

https://nevertoolatetostart.org

LEUKEMIA & LYMPHOMA SOCIETY

My name is Brandon M. Gidicsin. Every 10 minutes someone passes from blood cancer. I am honored to share that I am on a fundraising team led by my friend Tyler Sloane. Our team is "More Life". I am writing to ask for your support to help LLS in its mission to cure leukemia, lymphoma, Hodgkin's disease, and myeloma and improve the quality of life for patients and their families.

https://pages.lls.org/voy/li/li23/bgidicsin

CHILDREN'S HARBOR

Established in 1996, Children's Harbor is a nationally accredited nonprofit agency with a mission to provide a safe harbor and support to at risk children, youth, and families - keeping brothers and sisters together, strengthening families, and guiding youth towards independence.

https://www.childrensharbor.org

SAVE A SUIT

It's Not Just a Suit. It's a Fighting Chance. Save A Suit is a 501(c)(3) nonprofit organization that provides veterans and transitioning service members with business suits, professional attire, and other clothing resources they need to achieve job security.

https://www.saveasuit.org

BOYS TO MEN MENTORING VIRGINIA

Boys to Men Mentoring Network of Virginia (BTMVA) offers young men a safe place where they can talk about what is really going on in their lives, as well as a community of mentors and peers who listen, believe in them, and help them make better choices.

https://www.btmva.org

TECHGIRLZ

TechGirlz is a program of CompTIA Spark, a nonprofit social impact organization that focuses on unlocking the potential of the next generation by igniting their interest, confidence and skills in technology. It provides middle school girls with hands-on technology education, empowering them to solve real-world challenges and opening their minds to new opportunities. Since 2010, TechGirlz has served more than 40,000 middle school girls. This innovative program relies on partnerships with companies, organizations and community groups to deliver fun and engaging learning experiences as well as provide role models and community support. Working together, these efforts aim to bridge the gender gap in the tech industry to create a future where girls and women are equal participants in the digital world. Learn more at techgirlz.org.

PCS FOR PEOPLE

Owning a computer and having internet service shouldn't empty your wallet.

PCs for People provides refurbished computers to eligible customers for affordable prices. We also provide low-cost high-speed internet solutions. Through computers, internet, digital skills training, and technical support, we work to ensure everyone has an equal opportunity to reach their full potential through digital technology.

https://www.pcsforpeople.org

STEIGMANN PEACE AND TOLERANCE EDUCATION FUND

Rabbi Darren Levine and fellow members of the Tamid NYC (The Downtown Synagogue) congregation helped me establish *The Reghina, Nathan, and Sami Steigmann Family Peace and Tolerance Education Fund*.

The Fund enables me to share my life experience with audiences all over the world. Over the years, I have been honored to touch the hearts of thousands by sharing my unique message about hope, peace, and tolerance.

If you would like to bring me to your school, organization, or community, please contact Tamid NYC at "connect@tamidnyc.org" or contact me directly at "Sami1939@gmail.com." I am also on Facebook and would love to hear from you.

https://tamidnyc.org/sami

NOTES

_____

_____

_____

_____

_____

_____

_____

_____

_____

_____

_____

_____

_____

_____

_____

_____

_____

_____

_____

NOTES

_____

_____

_____

_____

_____

_____

_____

_____

_____

_____

_____

_____

_____

_____

_____

_____

_____

_____

_____

_____

_____

_____

PART 5: THE PATH FORWARD

NOTES

_____

_____

_____

_____

_____

_____

_____

_____

_____

_____

_____

_____

_____

_____

_____

_____

_____

_____

_____

_____

_____

THE NEXT STEP

Congratulations, you have almost finished this book. I hope by now you are excited about building self-awareness and enhancing your business networking skills.

I wrote this book to be a starting point for our relationship. As I see it, you have three opportunities in front of you right now.

- You can close this book and do nothing with the information I have shared. If you have gotten this far, I surely hope this is not an option.
- You can start building self-awareness and enhancing your business networking skills on your own, leveraging the tips, tactics, and strategies I have just given you.
- You can make the wise decision to join one of our weekly In This Together Roundtable sessions. There is no obligation. Signing up is super easy, and really, what do you have to lose? Maybe we are meant to work together. Maybe not. But we will not know unless you schedule a conversation. You can register to join our weekly sessions here https://inthistogetherroundtable.com/register

The choice is entirely up to you. Regardless of which path you take, I hope I have inspired you to start building self-awareness and enhancing your business networking skills on your own.

If I can be of service to you, please let me know and best wishes as you move forward.

Esther Deutsch
https://estherdeutsch.com

**Now, I have a question that I want you to ask yourself...
"what do you have to lose by taking action?"**

_____

_____

_____

_____

_____

_____

_____

_____

_____

_____

_____

_____

_____

_____

_____

_____

_____

NOTES

_____

_____

_____

_____

_____

_____

_____

_____

_____

_____

_____

_____

_____

_____

_____

_____

_____

_____

_____

NOTES

_____

_____

_____

_____

_____

_____

_____

_____

_____

_____

_____

_____

_____

_____

_____

_____

_____

_____

_____

_____

_____

NOTES

_____

_____

_____

_____

_____

_____

_____

_____

_____

_____

_____

_____

_____

_____

_____

_____

_____

_____

_____

NOTES

_____

_____

_____

_____

_____

_____

_____

_____

_____

_____

_____

_____

_____

_____

_____

_____

_____

_____

_____

_____

_____

ABOUT ESTHER DEUTSCH

A Social Worker and Operations Manager, Esther is very passionate about leadership development, education, and problem-solving through innovation.

She loves to network and build thriving communities by leading with heart, sparking creativity, and empowering individual team members to unite and take responsibility for collectively spreading an organization's mission and core purpose.

Her experiences include teaching adults and adolescents of all ages and abilities, founding and running multiple not-for-profit organizations, and producing various events and workshops for both the profit and not-for-profit sectors.

Esther currently works in Technology and Operations at RCS Professional Services and advises for a technology and Artificial Intelligence startup called marketintent.ai. She also co-hosts the "In This Together Roundtable" and offers 1-1 career coaching, Leadership, and LinkedIn optimization training.

Her favorite quote is:

"Leadership is a stance in the world. It's not a job title."

She is a big believer in the power of hard work and commitment.

ESTHER's CONTACT DETAILS:

https://estherdeutsch.com

https://www.linkedin.com/in/esther-deutsch

www.inthistogetherroundtable.com

https://www.youtube.com/channel/UCVy0Lqraxqrk3nRNO
gQeyBQ

https://www.instagram.com/rcsproservices

https://twitter.com/RCSProServices

https://www.linkedin.com/company/rcsprofessionalservices

https://www.facebook.com/RCSProServices

https://www.linkedin.com/company/in-this-together-
roundtable/about

NOTES

NOTES

Musings of a Networking Maven   82

NOTES

NOTES

_____

_____

_____

_____

_____

_____

_____

_____

_____

_____

_____

_____

_____

_____

_____

_____

_____

_____

_____

NOTES

NOTES

NOTES

NOTES

_____

_____

_____

_____

_____

_____

_____

_____

_____

_____

_____

_____

_____

_____

_____

_____

_____

_____

_____

_____

_____

NOTES

What were your biggest takeaways as you read this book?

_____

_____

_____

_____

_____

_____

_____

_____

_____

_____

_____

_____

_____

_____

_____

_____

_____

What questions do you have for me after reading this book?

_____

_____

_____

_____

_____

_____

_____

_____

_____

_____

_____

_____

_____

_____

_____

_____

_____

IN THIS TOGETHER ROUNDTABLE

In early 2020, businesspeople across the globe found themselves in the middle of a crisis. Our ability to conduct business through traditional channels became untenable, Lunches – out! In-person meetings, going to the office, water cooler conversations…even shaking hands were simply forbidden.

It was a scary time. We found ourselves on soggy ground. It was a time of tremendous stress.

In the middle of this crisis two people took it upon themselves to act, to bring businesspeople together again. Luke Van Every and Esther Deutsch picked a meeting time, invited some business associates to join them, and started to rebuild a business community that was truly lost at sea. This networking organization is the result of their genius and initiative.

In This Together Roundtable
Website

Scan the QR Code or go directly to our website here:

https://www.inthistogetherroundtable.com

www.ingramcontent.com/pod-product-compliance
Lightning Source LLC
Chambersburg PA
CBHW070807220526
45466CB00002B/585